MY LIFE IN THE WILD
CHEETAH

writer **Meredith Costain**   illustrator **Mick Posen**

RED
LEMON
PRESS

I am a cheetah.

I have a lean body with black spots and 'tear stripes' on my face. My home is the African grasslands. I run as fast as the wind. Let me tell you my story.

My brothers and I are born. I cannot see
my mother yet but I can smell her. I snuggle
into her warm tummy, drinking her milk.
She licks my wriggly brother clean
with her raspy tongue.

Each day I grow stronger and bigger.
My teeth grow longer and sharper.
But there are other animals on the prowl,
sniffing around, looking for dinner. Our mother
moves us around from place to place to keep us safe.

Every few days our mother leaves us
to go hunting. We stay in our nest, cuddled
together, our tummies rumbling with hunger.

Our ears prick up as we hear a chirping sound.
It's Mum, back from the hunt with our dinner.
We run to greet her, then join in the feast.

Learning to hunt is fun! We play together
every day, pouncing and jumping and
tripping each other up. We box
and wrestle and play tug-of-war.

Sometimes we chase small animals that Mum brings us, trapping them with our paws.

It's time for our first hunt. We follow
our mother as she patiently stalks
a herd of wildebeests, but we
soon lose interest.

My brothers start to play fight. Their noise alerts the animal our mother has chosen. It takes off across the plains. Mum speeds after it, then falls back, exhausted. The wildebeest escapes — for now.

The next day it's my turn. I choose a small gazelle, away from its herd. Then I wait. And watch.

I slink forward. The gazelle lifts its head and sniffs the air. I freeze. Then, slowly, silently, I creep towards it again.

Closer... closer... until finally...

I pounce! The gazelle leaps in fright,
then bounds away, zigzagging across
the grassy plain. I twist and turn
as I dash after it, trying my best
not to trip or fall.

Then I bring it down with a swipe of my paw.

I lie in the grass, puffing and panting.
I'm too tired to eat right now. I drag
the gazelle back to our den.

Later, three hungry hyenas come sniffing around. My mother helps my brothers chase them away.

Time passes. Our mother moves on to a new hunting ground, leaving us to look after ourselves. My brothers and I still practise our charging and pouncing. I am the fastest runner – and the best hunter!

It is time for me
to leave my brothers.
They will stay together,
helping each other hunt.
I set out across the wide plains,
looking for a hunting ground of my own.

I have found a new home, far away from my old one.
I saw my mother once, chasing a gazelle.
But I never saw my brothers again.

These days, I don't have time
to play. Now that I have my own family,
it's time for me to teach
them all to hunt!

Did You Know?

Cheetahs usually give birth to three to five cubs.

First they make a nest for their cubs in a quiet, hidden spot, such as tall grass. Cubs are blind when they are born. They begin crawling around the nest at four to ten days old, when their eyes finally open. Before then, they use touch and scent to find their mother's milk.

The mother cheetah moves her cubs for safety.

The mother hides her cubs in long grass, under bushes or among rocks while she goes off to hunt. Every few days she moves her cubs to a different place, so their scent does not build up and attract predators.

Cheetahs make many different sounds.

A mother calling her cubs gives a high-pitched, bird-like chirp, which can be heard from far away. Cheetahs also use this sound when greeting each other. They purr like a cat when content, bleat when in distress and growl or hiss when attacking or defending themselves.

Cubs prepare for life by playing.

Cubs learn how to hunt for themselves through play. They practice pouncing, stalking and ambushing each other or small animals their mother brings them. Playing also helps them grow stronger and move their bodies well.

Cheetahs can run fast, but not for long.

A cheetah can only sprint for about 30 seconds before it runs out of energy. If its prey can stay out of reach for that long, it may be able to escape. Only about half of a cheetah's chases are successful.

Cheetahs choose and stalk their prey.

Cheetahs move almost silently when they are hunting. This allows them to get as close to their prey as they can before starting the chase. They look out for an animal that is small, weak, old or separated from the herd, to increase their chances of catching it.

Did You Know? (continued)

The fastest animal on land is the cheetah.

Cheetahs are built for speed, with lean bodies, flexible spines and hips and large, strong hearts and lungs. Their short, blunt claws grip the ground as they run, like the spikes on a pair of golf shoes. Having a long tail helps them keep their balance during sharp turns.

After hunting, cheetahs can be too exhausted to eat.

Once they have caught their prey, cheetahs are often too tired to eat right away. Instead, they hide it in a safe place. If undisturbed by vultures, hyenas or lions, cheetahs can spend the whole day eating.

The mother cheetah moves on to start a new family.

The mother leaves her cubs when they are about 18 months old, to start another family. The cubs stay together for about another six months, practising their hunting skills.

Male and female cheetahs live separately.

Female cheetahs leave their male siblings at around two years of age and set up their own territory, called the 'home range'. The males stay together in small groups for the rest of their lives.

The cheetah's tail has spots, black rings and a white tip.

When moving her cubs through long grass, the mother cheetah raises her tail. Its bright white tip acts as a marker to help the cubs keep her in sight.

Meet the Cat Family

Cheetahs are part of the cat family.
Here are some other family members.

Jaguar

Lion cubs are born
with brown spots on
their bodies, which fade
as they grow older.

Pride of lions

Serval

QUIZ

1. How many different kinds of cats
   can you see here?

2. Which cat has a mane?

3. Which cat has the most stripes?

4. Which cat has a small head
   and large ears?

Cheetah

Scientific name: *Acinonyx jubatus*

Coat colour: tan with black spots and a white belly

Body length: 122 centimetres (4 ft)

Weight: 31–63 kilograms (69–140 lbs)

Shoulder height: 76+ centimetres (30+ in)

Tail length: 72 centimetres (28.5 in)

Top speed: 112 km/h (70 mph)

Acceleration: 0 to 84 kilometres per hour (0 to 52 mph) in 3 seconds

Conservation status: endangered

Habitat: small pockets of Africa

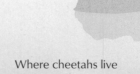

Where cheetahs live

AFRICA

Margay

Tiger

Lynx

5. How many have long tails?

6. How many have short tails?

7. Which of these cats looks the most like a cheetah?

8. Which cat has tufts on its ears?

Glossary

ambush   to hide, then attack

cub   a baby of a cheetah or other large cat

escape   to get away from danger

exhausted   very tired

mane   longer hair along the neck or head

predator   an animal that hunts

prey   an animal hunted as food

pride   a family or group of lions

sibling   a brother or sister

sprint   to quickly run a short distance

stalk   to follow quietly and secretly

territory   area where a group of animals lives

RED LEMON PRESS

Published in the UK by:
Red Lemon Press (An imprint of Weldon Owen)
Deepdene Lodge,
Deepdene Avenue,
Dorking,
Surrey RH5 4AT
www.weldonowen.co.uk

Conceived and produced by
Weldon Owen Pty Ltd
Ground Floor 42–44 Victoria Street, McMahons Point
Sydney NSW 2060, Australia
weldonowenpublishing.com

Copyright © 2012 Weldon Owen Pty Ltd

WELDON OWEN PTY LTD

Managing Director Kay Scarlett
Publisher Corinne Roberts
Creative Director Sue Burk
Senior Vice President,
International Sales Stuart Laurence
Sales Manager, North America Ellen Towell
Administration Manager,
International Sales Kristine Ravn

Managing Editor Helen Bateman
Consultant Professor Phil Whitfield
Design Concept Cooling Brown Ltd
Designer Gabrielle Green
Images Manager Trucie Henderson
Production Director Todd Rechner
Production and Prepress Controller Mike Crowton
Illustrations Mick Posen/The Art Agency
except Meet the Cat Family pages.

ISBN: 978-1-78342-143-5

Printed and bound in China.

A WELDON OWEN PRODUCTION